The

Simple

Sabbat

The

Simple Sabbat

A Family Friendly Approach

To The Eight Pagan Holidays

M. Flora Peterson

3

First Edition, 2011

"The Words of the Star Goddess" by Zsuzsanna Budapest used with permission

Published by M. "Flora" Peterson and FloraSage Therapies
Photograph of Author by Eagle Eye Photography – G. Peterson
Cover Design: Beth Nichols

ISBN-13: 978-1460938089
ISBN-10: 1460938089

What People Are Saying About

The Simple Sabbat

"This book is a must have for every Pagan household!"
Melanie Wallace ~ Founder and Creator of "One Ascension"

"Flora is the goddess of flowers, and flowers are the language of the goddess. Flowers say Love. Flora puts a little bit of happy into every day by following a spiritual path that has lightheartedness and hope. She is practical minded and easy going, and fills the pages of her book with good ideas to engage with the planet and the soul."
Zsuzsanna Budapest ~ Founder of the Woman's Spirituality Movement and Dianic Tradition

"What Flora has written here is treasure trove of much needed practical information. As an Earth Based Spiritualist with a busy and fast paced life, this will be my "Go-To" reference and practical guide book for all Sabbat activities throughout the year. One of the many things that I love

about Flora is that she has the unique ability to make spiritual advice accessible to everyone. She has succeeded in writing a useful and no-nonsense handbook for the wheel of the year. Flora has been a personal inspiration and is always the consummate expert at giving stimulating, valuable and informative spiritual advice while influencing me in countless ways. With this book, she has, once again, delivered and surpassed these expectations! Thank you, Flora."
Hibiscus Moon ~ Hibiscus Moon Crystal Academy Founder

Dedication

This book is dedicated to my children who have taught me how to have fun, no matter what! And how to see the simplistic joy in everything around me. Yay!!! It is also dedicated to Máiréad Nesbitt for reminding my soul how to dance.

About the Author

Creator of The Yay Factor™ life coaching program, Flora is also an intuitive teacher and consultant. Flora has trained directly with Z. Budapest and Sonia Choquette, and is internationally regarded for her instructional videos on YouTube under the channel name of "CharmingPixieFlora". She empowers her viewers and clients by teaching them to embrace all that works for them, and to hone in on their own skills and inner truth to create a unique path for themselves. Flora is driven to help teach people how to truly live life to the fullest using her gifts of intuition and spirit filled teaching techniques.

Flora resides in Oklahoma with her husband, four children, two cats and two dogs "Teddy" and "Marley".

Acknowledgements

To my husband whose dedication to me, no matter how hyper I get, is never-ending. To my father for showing me that being a steward to this land is something to be proud of. To my sister Michele for taking the time to hear and understand my passion about my path, I am truly grateful. To my dearest friend and sister in the Goddess Melanie Wallace, who is a constant source of strength for me and reminds me to connect with the divine *One* source on a daily basis.

To Bobbie Grennier who has spent hours on Skype with me discussing everything under the sun to help me make sense of life during times of chaos; I truly appreciate your honesty and candor, you are priceless. To Z. Budapest and all my Coven sisters in the Susan B. Anthony Coven Number 1, for being there for me when times got tough and always reminding me why I do what I do. To the great and powerful Lady Ro from the frozen land to the north whose cosmic connection runs so very deep. I honor you! To Candace D. for being such a genuine and honest force in the online community, I truly admire you. To Hibiscus Moon for your high level of constant professionalism in the online community, I truly look up to you.

To all of my clients who allow me to live my dream of teaching and empowering people on a daily basis. To all my viewers on YouTube who have encouraged me along the way...Yay!!!

To my cosmic sisters Deb, Leta, Naty, and Cathy, our circle of sisterhood means the world to me. Yay!!! To Gail who has been there for me whenever I am in need of a steady sounding board and a level head, I am truly grateful for you. To all teachers and mentors, past and present in my life who instilled in me the desire to question everything and not stop until I feel 100% sure that I am living my authentic life.

To Teddy, my Chihuahua, who kept my lap warm during the writing of this book. To JoJo, Emily, Kristin, Kody and all the other fabulous folks at Starbucks that kept me fueled during the many hours of writing this book. To Beth Nichols for all your curiosity about my beliefs which helped to fuel my drive for this book as well as believing in me during this project. Thank you so much. And last but not least to you, the reader, for finding what I do helpful enough to buy this book. Many Blessings to you!

Contents

*P*rologue

On October 22, 1987, I began to get intuitive messages from the Divine, which was also the day my mother passed away; I was 12 years old. Soon after that I began to frequent new age shops to try and learn about this wonderfully crazy ability that literally just popped into my head. One day, while browsing the shelves at a local book store, I made my way to the new age section, and a book caught my eye… "Earth Magic" by Marion Weinstein. I didn't recall seeing it before but something inside told me I had to have this book. I devoured it within two days. I finally discovered who *I* was; I discovered I was a *Witch*.

I bought and read every book I could get my hands on about Witchcraft, some were great, and others were not. One thing I noticed was that most of them had the same information surrounded by a whole lot of "fluff." I finally sought out a teacher and learned more with her than I ever did out of a book.

It was during that process that I realized that magic and being Pagan didn't have to be as hard as it was portrayed in some books, it really is so very simple and natural. It is about connecting to the elements, the basic building blocks of the universe, and the universal laws to create our lives. This path seemed so natural and so fluid; like I was remembering something I once did a lifetime ago. Many things were as natural as breathing, I had already been doing them for years.

Once I started to learn the craft, I shared what I learned with my kids. We learned the craft together and made it a family affair. In May of 2009, I started my YouTube channel, "CharmingPixieFlora" in which I shared and taught my family path to those who cared to watch. I was shocked and thrilled at how many people wrote to me telling me that my fresh approach to Paganism had revitalized their own Pagan practice. Yay!!! Soon after I started my channel I began taking students for *Year and a Day* studies and found that my simple method of teaching was just what they were looking for.

When I started writing this book, I didn't want it to be just another Sabbat book; I wanted it to be a simple and useable book for everyone. I hope you enjoy this simple approach to the eight holy days of the Wheel of the Year.

Introduction

This book is for those of you who have a basic understanding and knowledge of the Wheel of the Year but may not have the time to plan a ritual circle or Sabbat. This book is a compilation of simple and very eclectic Sabbat rituals, recipes and crafting ideas that anyone can use to celebrate the eight Pagan holidays. These are rituals and ideas that my family and I personally use yearly, and have found that they are a great way to connect to the seasons in nature and the turning of the Wheel. In the instance where I have made instructional videos on YouTube, I will post the link below the instructions, as I know that some individuals learn better by seeing rather than reading.

My goal while writing this book, was to make it as simple as possible without a lot of "fluff". So that one can simply pull out the book, turn to the Sabbat that is forthcoming and make a simple yet powerful ritual. That is also the reason for this books diminutive size; to make it as portable as possible.

This book is also set up so that children of any age can help with the rituals, crafts and activities if they would like. This can be a great teaching tool for parents to use to help teach their children about these special days.

Please know that this is only touching the surface of these holy days and is not meant to be an in-depth study or comprehensive list. It is only meant to act as a spring board for you, your family or group in hopes that you will eventually create your own hand crafted Sabbat rituals and traditions. I am hoping this will be enough to get you started on a long and joyous journey of the Wheel of the Year.

In Perfect Love and Perfect Trust,

M. Flora Peterson

Chapter 1

The Wheel of the Year

The simple Sabbat. A Sabbat is a Pagan holy day or holiday that marks the changing of the seasons. It is a time when Pagan's all around the world gather to celebrate the turning of the Wheel of the Year. These holidays are based on the Sun's rotational cycle, or Sun cycle. Pick up any Farmer's Almanac and look inside for an Equinox or Solstice and you will surely find it. These seasonal occurrences mark a very powerful time for those in agricultural societies as an ideal time for planting and harvesting. These four events also mark four of the eight Pagan holidays.

The other four holidays are the cross-quarter days, the times between the equinox and solstice, which mark changes in the natural world around us. These holidays honor the cycles in nature and in all of life. By honoring the changing seasons and connecting to the natural life cycles, we in turn, honor ourselves. Once you start to pay attention to the changes that happen all around you in the natural world, it is so much easier to feel the connection between your Spirit and the spirits of the great Divine.

Here is a list of each of the holidays in the Sun cycle, or The Wheel of the Year, and the dates in which they are typically celebrated.

The Wheel of the Year
Northern Hemisphere (N.H.)

- Yule / Winter Solstice – December 21 – 23

- Candlemas – February 2

- Ostara / Spring Equinox – March 21 – 23

- Beltane – May 1

- Summer Solstice / Litha – June 21 – 23

- Lammas – August 1

- Mabon / Fall Equinox – September 21 – 23

- Samhain – October 31

The Wheel of the Year
Southern Hemisphere (S.H)

🌀 Yule / Winter Solstice – June 21 – 23

🌀 Candlemas – August 1

🌀 Ostara / Spring Equinox – September 21 – 23

🌀 Beltane – October 31

🌀 Summer Solstice / Litha – December 21 – 23

🌀 Lammas – February 2

🌀 Mabon / Fall Equinox – March 21 – 23

🌀 Samhain – May 1

Sabbats are part of a celebration that can last all week, all day, an hour or for a few minutes, and are conducted in a ritual circle or special sacred space. In chapter two, I discuss the ritual and circle formats used for these holidays. In the chapters following that, there is a brief explanation of each Sabbat along with activities for the whole family to participate in. I encourage you, your family, your coven or your group to become familiar with them before you start planning your celebration.

~ Notes ~

Chapter 2

Ritual Circle Formats

Sabbats are very special days, akin to Easter and Christmas, with all the trimmings and accoutrements. At some point during these days a ritual is held along with much feasting and many activities.

In this chapter, I give you examples of the two main ritual circle formats I use with my family: the *Full Circle* and *Simple Circle* formats as well as a *Simple Sabbat Ritual* format that you can use when you don't have time to do an elaborate Sabbat ritual.

The *Full Circle* format gives you step-by-step instructions on how to construct and deconstruct a sacred circle for ritual. This circle format is longer and more in depth then the *Simple Circle* format, which is just a shell of the full circle. The

Simple Circle I recommend for families with young children who may not have a long attention span or someone who may not have a lot of time that they can devote to the Sabbat, but still want to do a ritual.

I encourage you to read each of them over before your ritual and make any changes you feel would be appropriate. For example, my family has the four elemental directions as:

- East ~ Earth
- South ~ Fire
- West ~ Water
- North ~ Air

If the directions for your family or tradition are different, then modify accordingly. My family does not call in the element of Spirit as we believe that through breath we are always consciously connected with Spirit in our heart space. So Spirit is always present with us.

At the end of each chapter I have a prepared ritual for the Sabbat just discussed which lists all the items you will need. I encourage you to gather your everyday ritual items and keep them together in a special place, so when the time comes to do ritual you have them ready to go. These items may include things such as:

- A Pentacle or your family's sacred symbol
- Goblet and plate for cakes and ale
- Libation bowl if ritual is performed inside
- Representations of the Goddess and God
- Representations of each of the Elements

These basic items will be referred to in the list at the end of the chapter as "usual ritual items."

Full Circle Format

Clear the ritual space: The ritual space must first be prepared by clearing it of any unwanted energies. While doing this, use visualization to envision the area being energetically cleansed. This can be done using various techniques:

- Light an incense or smudge stick and walk the circle once deosil or clockwise to cleanse the circle
- Use a shaker once around the space
- Take a besom or broom and "sweep" away any unwanted energies from the ritual space
- Use only intention to clear the area
- Vacuum or sweep the area if conducting ritual inside

Set up altar: An altar can be set up using a table, log, stones or on a blanket that has been laid on the ground. Set up your altar facing in a direction comfortable with your tradition or family, with all of the items needed for the upcoming ritual. My family sets up the ritual altar facing east.

Ground and center your energy: When you are in a sacred circle, you must fully be present in what you are doing. To ground and center your energy, start by taking three deep breaths and turning your energy to your heart center. Release the day and release all but your ritual intentions while in this sacred space. When you feel you are ready, proceed.

Casting the circle: To cast an energetic circle, walk around your sacred space in the direction you feel is correct, either clockwise or counter clockwise, three times as you say "Light above, light below, Spirits guide me in this glow, as above, so below." As you do this, envision energy rising from the Earth and surrounding you in a sphere of light.

Seal the circle: Sealing a circle is essentially creating a vacuum so that no unwanted energies can enter the circle while you are conducting your ritual. To seal the circle simply say: "As above so below, this circle is now sealed." Some traditions require you to 'cut' a doorway if you leave the sacred space after it is sealed. Discuss this with your group or family and decide how you feel about this practice and adjust accordingly.

Call upon the four quarters: Invite the four directional elements to be with you during your ritual if you choose. While you call them in, you can light the directional candles and incense or put out a symbol that will represent each element for you:

⊚ **East:** Facing the direction of east, raise arms and say: "Hail spirits and guardians of the East, element of Earth. Bring us your gifts of stability, new beginnings , and confidence. Oh morning star. We call you forth to this circle, that you may grant us your protection and wisdom. Hail."

- ๑ **South:** Facing the direction of south, raise arms and say: "Hail spirits and guardians of the South, element of Fire. Bring us your gifts of will, courage, and action. We call you forth to this circle, that you may grant us your protection and wisdom. Hail."

- ๑ **West:** Facing the direction of west, raise arms and say: "Hail spirits and guardians of the West, element of Water. Bring us your gifts of emotion, serenity, and compassion. Oh evening star. We call you forth to this circle, that you may grant us your protection and wisdom. Hail."

- ๑ **North:** Facing the direction of north, raise arms and say: "Hail spirits and guardians of the North, element of Air. Bring us your gifts of inspiration, mental clarity, and instinct. We call you forth to this circle, that you may grant us your protection and wisdom. Hail."

Anointing with oil: Anoint your third eye and hands with oil while saying the following: "I, (name) am consecrated in the names of the Goddess and the God, in this circle." [Use any oil you enjoy to use. If you don't have any prepared oils you can simply use water or olive oil.]

Invocation of the Goddess: Invite the Goddess to be present in the circle. Light the Goddess candle, raise arms in the direction of above and say: "I call you down great Goddess – Maiden, Mother and Crone to enter this circle. Be with us now, in accordance with freewill and the good of all. So Mote It Be."

Charge of the Goddess:

⊚ **The Words of the Star Goddess***
By Zsuzanna Budapest (www.zbudapest.com)

"I am the beauty of the green earth,
The white moon among the stars;
The mystery of the deep waters, the desire of human heart,
Know the Mystery, therefore....
That if ye find not what ye seek within,
Ye shall never find it without.
Lo, I have been with you from the beginning,
And I am whom ye will find at the end of your desire."

Used with permission

Invocation of the God: Invite the God to be present in the circle. Light the God candle, raise arms in the direction of above and say: "I call you down great God - Boy, Father, and Sage to enter this circle. Be with us now, in accordance with freewill and the good of all. So Must It Be."

Charge of the God:

⊚ **The Words of the Star God** (adapted from The Words of the Star Goddess)
By M. Flora Peterson

"I am the lust of the wild animal,
The bright sun among the sky;
The mystery of the water's flow,

The root of all things primal,
Know the Mystery, therefore….
That if ye cherish not what ye seek within,
Ye shall never find it without.
Honor with reverence the Mother Gaia with love and compassion,
Then ye will know the great Mystery within through peace."

Insert: This is where you insert your planned:

- Esbat
- Sabbat
- Special ritual (ie… Dedication, Initiation, Naming, Coming of Age etc.)
- Spell

Cone of power: The cone of power is when the power and intentions raised during the ritual are sent out to the universe to begin working. If in a group, join palms side by side with finger tips pointing to the sky to create the cone. If alone, raise hands in front of you (raised about shoulder height) and envision the cone. Envision a clockwise vortex of power in the shape of a cone, (or upside down ice cream cone) spinning faster and faster. Raise your hands higher until you feel the power is at its peak. When the power is at its height and you feel it is time, burst and release the cone of power to set the spell or intention in motion. Do this by simply envisioning the cone explode into tiny drops of sparkling energy. Envision the energy floating down to the earth wherever it needs to go for your spell or intentions to manifest.

Proceed with cakes and ale: Partaking of food and drink at this time, will help your body recover from channeling universal energy that was used in the intention or spell portion of your ritual, this can consist of any type of food and drink. Be sure to offer some of the food and drink to the God and Goddess before you consume as an offering of honor to them by simply placing or pouring it on the Earth. If you are conducting ritual inside you can have a bowl reserved especially for this libation.

As you give the cakes to everyone in the circle say, "May you never hunger" - they repeat it back to you.

As you give the ale or drink to everyone in the circle say, "May you never thirst" - they repeat it back to you.

Relax and chat a bit: This is where some covens or groups may differ on etiquette. Some groups are very serious and do not allow joking or merriment in circle, others encourage it. The more serious groups will begin to deconstruct the circle at this point; the groups that allow for some good humor and fun will usually improvise during this time in the ritual.

If you are a solitary, this is the perfect time to just sit and enjoy the energy of the ritual space and be with essence of the elements and the God and Goddess.

Once your merriment or time in the circle has come to a nice lull, it is time to bid farewell to the Goddess, God, and the elements as well as disperse any remaining energies.

Thank and bid farewell to the Goddess: Raising arms in the direction of above, say: "Thank you great Goddess, for your guidance and protection on this circle; for your wisdom and your gifts. Go if you must, stay if you'd like. Hail and farewell."

Thank and bid farewell to the God: Raising arms in the direction of above, say: "Thank you great God, for your guidance and protection on this circle; for your wisdom and your gifts. Go if you must, stay if you'd like. Hail and farewell."

Thank and release the quarters: Release the quarters in the reverse order that you called them into the circle. Facing the respective directions with arms raised up, say: "Spirits and guardians of the (North, West, South and East) element of (Air, Water, Fire and Earth) thank you for your protection on this circle; for your wisdom and your gifts. Go if you must, stay if you'd like. Hail and farewell."

Open the circle: To open the circle and sink the energy contained in the sphere of light back to the earth, start by simply walking widdershins or counter clockwise, starting in the North. With every step, visualize the sphere of light growing dimmer and going back into the earth as you say: "Light above, light below. This glow around me is free to go. As above so below. The circle is open, but never broken. Merry meet and merry part, until we merry meet again. So Mote It Be."

Ground and center: With your hands out at your sides, palms facing down slowly start to sit. As you sit envision the excess magical energy that has built up in your body during this ritual slowly going into the earth, (you will not lose any personal energy during this). Place your hands on either side of you on the earth, close your eyes and concentrate on the excess magical energy draining from you. Once you feel all the excess energy is dispersed, it is done.

Gather items and clear area: You should then clear the area of any excess energy in a similar manner as what you did to prepare the area for ritual. Use a shaker or broom in the circle once around to disperse any remaining energy.

If ritual was done inside take the libation bowl outside and pour the libation out on the ground.

Simple Circle Format

Prepare ritual space and set up altar with all items needed for ritual.

"Light above, Light below, Spirits guide us in this glow, as above, so below. As above so below, this circle is now sealed."

Call upon the quarters and light the directional candles and incense.

"Hail spirits of the East, Element of Earth. Be with us now."
"Hail spirits of the South, Element of Fire. Be with us now."
"Hail spirits of the West, Element of Water. Be with us now."
"Hail spirits of the North, Element of Air. Be with us now."

Invocation of the Goddess:
"I call you down great Goddess be with us now as we work magic, in accordance with freewill and the good of all. So Mote It Be."

Invocation of the God:
"I call you down great God be with us now as we work magic, in accordance with freewill and the good of all. So Must It Be."

Insert: Esbat ~ Sabbat ~ Spell ~ Special ritual

Raise the Cone of Power

Cakes and wine: "May you never hunger" ~ "May you never thirst"

Thank and bid farewell to the Goddess: "Thank you great Goddess. Go if you must, stay if you'd like. Hail and farewell."

Thank and bid farewell to the God: "Thank you great God. Go if you must, stay if you'd like. Hail and farewell."

Thank and release the quarters: "Spirits and guardians of the (North, West, South and East) element of (Air, Water, Fire and Earth) thank you for your protection on this circle. Go if you must, stay if you'd like. Hail and farewell."

"Light above, light below. This glow around us is free to go. As above so below. The circle is open, but never broken. Merry meet and merry part, until we merry meet again. So Mote It Be."

Ground and center – Gather items and clear the area.

Shaker the circle once to disperse any remaining energy.

Simple Sabbat Ritual Format

Begin ritual with the *Simple Circle* format.

In the portion of the format where you insert your Sabbat ritual you can explain the season and the meaning of this time of year and what it represents.

Discuss the current God and Goddess aspects in nature.

Pick the activities to do in the amount of time you have in your circle.

Finish ritual with the remaining *Simple Circle* format.

[Author's note - I use the Goddess and God in each of my rituals, if your group, family or tradition uses just the Goddess or God, respectfully, please adjust your ritual accordingly.]

~ Notes ~

~ Notes ~

~ Notes ~

Chapter 3

Yule

Time – N.H. ~ When the Sun is in 1 degree of Capricorn – December 21 – 23 / S.H ~ When the Sun is in 1 degree of Cancer – June 21 – 23.

Meaning of the Season - This celebration honors the longest night and shortest day of the year. It's also the time the Sun God is born again. For some Witches this is considered the New Year. The Sun will start waxing or growing from this day forward. Dating back over 12,000 years, this is one of the most celebrated times in history.

God - The God is a baby born of the Goddess. This is also when the Holly King and Oak King do battle to see who will rule the next half of the year.

Goddess - This is the time of year the Goddess is in the Mother aspect and she gives birth to the Sun God.

Colors – Any colors you see in nature can be used at this time, such as green and red from the holly bush and evergreens. You can also use gold and yellow to represent the fiery Sun that will be born on this day.

Altar – The Gaia or Mother Mary statue can be used as well as Sun representations. Bring in evergreens, candles and all kinds of colorful items for this altar.

Activities – Here is a small list of things that can be done to celebrate this joyous day. I encourage you to look for more things to add to this list.

- Put up a Yule tree in your home to remind all who enter about the lush summer months
- Watch the Sun rise and set
- Make a bonfire
- Stay up all night to keep a vigil during the Goddesses labor
- Create New Year's or Solstice spell bags
- Sing carols
- Put candles in the windows
- Make maracas
- Create cinnamon and applesauce ornaments
- Have a Holly King and Oak King dual

- Make a pickle ornament out of clay and hide it in the Yule tree, whoever finds it in the morning will get an extra gift (Yay!)
- Create a Yule log with either a tree stump or out of cake; this is also called a *Bouche Noel*
- Ring bells to hail the dawn
- Put out seeds and nuts for the animals
- Bake Solstice cakes and give them to your neighbors

Incense

This is a very versatile recipe, use the amounts of each ingredient that you are called to use. Combine all ingredients into a glass container and burn on a charcoal block or in a bonfire during the celebration of the Yule season.

- Bay leaves broken up into pieces
- Red sandalwood powder
- Frankincense resin
- Myrrh resin
- Three pine needles
- One naturally fallen spider (one that has died naturally)

YouTube video at the following link:
http://www.youtube.com/watch?v=cIm8338ygxs

Oil

In a ½ oz. clean glass bottle, fill up to the shoulder with jojoba or other carrier oil. Add the following essential oils and ingredients to the bottle.

- ๑ 3 drops rosemary essential oil
- ๑ 2 drops frankincense essential oil
- ๑ 1 drop sandalwood essential oil
- ๑ 1 pine needle
- ๑ 1 citrine chip

YouTube video at the following link:
http://www.youtube.com/watch?v=cIm8338ygxs

Solstice Cakes

This is one of my favorite cakes to make and you will soon see why. These are a bit time consuming, but are so worth it. These diminutive cakes rarely last for more than a few days in my house; as with the Sun at this time, here today – gone tomorrow.

Ingredients for topping:
- ๑ ¾ cup butter softened or butter substitute
- ๑ ¾ cup brown sugar packed
- ๑ 2 cans of pineapple rounds

Ingredients for filling:
- ๑ ½ tub of cream cheese (real or non-dairy both are fantastic for this recipe)
- ๑ ¼ cup mandarin oranges drained

Ingredients for cake:
- ๑ 1 box yellow cake mix + necessary ingredients (see box)
- ๑ High pulp orange juice (enough to replace the liquid for the box mix)

Preheat oven to 350°F. Grease cupcake tins and set aside. Mix together brown sugar and butter until thoroughly combined. Place a spoonful of topping into tins, dividing evenly among the cupcake tins. Drain pineapple rounds and place one slice in each cup. If the slice is too big, tear off of a piece of the round and use in another cup. Keep going until all the cups are full. Set aside.

Place cream cheese into a small bowl, stir until smooth. In a blender or food processor blend the mandarin oranges until just broken up, a few seconds will do. Stir together the oranges and the cream cheese until blended.

Empty contents of yellow cake mix into bowl, combine the ingredients called for on the box EXCEPT for the liquid. Replace the liquid (water) portion with high pulp orange juice. Mix as directed on the box.

Fill the cups with cake batter until ¾ full. You may have extra batter, if you do; you can make a separate mini cake.

Take the orange/cream cheese filling and spoon a small amount into the center of each cake dividing evenly.

Place tins in the center of the oven and bake for 20 - 25 minutes.

Once finished, take tins out and place on cooling rack. While cakes are cooling, take a knife and cut around each cake to ensure they will slide out later. After you loosen the edges take a cookie sheet, place on top of cupcake tins and invert. Leave until completely cooled. The cakes should slide out of the tin and onto the sheet.

YouTube Video at the following link.
http://www.youtube.com/watch?v=LuPWPIYowiM

New Year's / Solstice Spell Bags

The Winter Solstice is a time of new beginnings and a fresh start. After the dark and waning period of the year, the Sun now starts to wax and become stronger. This is a great time to think about the things you accomplished over the last year. What did you set into motion and what manifested? This is the perfect time to think about what you want to have manifest for the next year in your life. With your reflections and intentions set; a fun way to ring in the New Year on Solstice morning is with the help of an Air spell in the form of a New Year's Spell bag.

Items needed:
- Various colors of paper lunch bags
- Decorations for the outside such as glue, glitter, and stickers
- Intentions to infuse into the decoration and creation of the bag

Decorate the outside of the bag taking time to really think about your intentions for the upcoming year. Once the Sun rises on Solstice morning, fill your bag with your intentions and your spell with a whisper, blow up and pop at the Sun's first light rays of the year. Yay!!!

YouTube video at the following link.
http://www.youtube.com/watch?v=iDukZc78_m4

Maracas

It seems everywhere we turn this time of year and everywhere we go, someone is celebrating and having some type of holiday party. This is the time of year when the Goddess labors all night long on Solstice eve, and finally gives birth to the Sun God at the break of dawn. Every birth deserves a festive celebration and joyous merriment. What would a party and celebration be without maracas? To liven up your Solstice celebration, make these fun and easy maracas to help ring in the new year and the birth of the Sun God.

Items needed:
- Two toilet paper rolls or one paper towel roll cut in two
- Two light bulbs (not halogen)
- Glue
- Water
- Newspaper strips
- Tissue (to stuff the handle with)
- Paint

Cut newspaper strips into manageable pieces (around 2 x 6 inches long). Mix the glue and water to a consistency of 2 parts glue to 1 part water.

With your non-dominant hand hold the paper tube, then place the light bulb in the top of the tube. Hold the bulb in place with your holding hand index finger. With your free hand stuff the other end of the paper tube with tissue until it's full.

Dip the newspaper strips into the glue mixture and start to paper mache the light bulb and tube until you have covered it completely. Set on a baking rack until dry. Repeat paper mache process three to four times.

Once you have three or four coats of paper mache on the maraca, and it is completely dry, carefully tap the light bulb end on a hard surface until light bulb breaks, this will be the "shaker" side of your maraca. (If you tap too hard, you may break or crack the paper mache layers.)

Once you have cracked the bulb, now it's time to paint and decorate your maraca.

YouTube Video at the following link.
http://www.youtube.com/watch?v=ECnYUtKaTvo

Yule Sabbat – Full Ritual

Items for ritual:

- One white small taper candle
- One red small taper candle
- One black small taper candle
- A Goddess and God Candle
- A second God candle
- Musical instruments such as maracas, tambourines, and drums
- Pinecones
- Oak King statue or representation

- ๑ Holly King statue or representation
- ๑ Red or green table cloth
- ๑ Usual ritual items

Insert into ritual circle format

Ring bell:

"Behold the season of Yule. Blessed be the Goddess who gives birth to the God on this night. Blessed be to the newborn God."

Ring bell:

"The Holly King who has grown old guarding over the land since Summer Solstice does not want to give up his guardianship over this realm to the newborn Oak King. They must battle to see who will reign the next turning of the wheel."

Act out a dual between the Oak King and Holly King:

"The Holly King has lost this battle and retreats. As he departs, he leaves gifts for all his beloved creatures as symbols of his love. He is carried away to the other realm by his mighty team of stags where he will await for the Summer Solstice, a time when he is at the height of his strength. Farewell old Holly King, until next Solstice, we bid you farewell."

Extinguish God candle:

Remove the Holly King horn and extinguished God candle off of the altar and replace it with the Oak King representation and new God candle.

Ring bell once and light the new God candle:

"We welcome the Oak King, who comes to us in the darkest of nights on this Winter Solstice. Through this mystery of death and rebirth, we are reminded of the promise of nature; that which is born, lives and dies, will surely be born again from the womb of the Goddess. We welcome the New Year through the birth of the light and Sun. All hail the Sun God tonight!"

Ring bell:

Take the Goddess candle in your left hand and the God candle in your right hand. Or have two participants each hold the base of one of the candles.

"Tonight the Goddess and God are reunited. Tonight life begins again, and the light begins to get stronger. Blessed be the light. Blessed be the divine force of creation."

Move flames together so they are one. Let them be one for a few minutes. Place back on altar in their respective places.

Motion to the white, red and black candles as you say:

"Behold these three candles; the white, which represents the beginning of all things, the red candle that represents the middle of all things and the height of all projects in our lives and finally we have the black candle, a symbol for things that are ending and are ready to go back to the cauldron of rebirth."

Light the white candle:

"Blessed be the Maiden, innocent and fresh. Blessed be the Boy, joyous and inspirational."

Light the red candle:

"Blessed be the Mother, fertile and loving. Blessed be the Father, abundant and nurturing."

Light the black candle:

"Blessed be the Crone, powerful and wise. Blessed be the Sage, protector and guide."

Ring bell:

"Blessed be the Triple Goddess, Blessed be the Triple God."

"Now is the time of great celebration and joy, let us make lots of music to wake up the Earth to announce the arrival of the Sun God." (Use maracas, tambourines, drums, voices or anything to make lots of fun noises.)

Sing a few Yule songs

[Finish ritual with the format chosen from chapter 2]

~ Notes ~

~ Notes ~

~ Notes ~

Chapter 4

Candlemas ~ Imbolc

Time – N.H. ~ When the Sun is in 15 degrees of Aquarius – February 1 – 3 / S.H. ~ When the Sun is in 15 degrees of Leo – August 1 – 3.

Meaning of the Season – The stirring of the Earth begins, the seeds below are drinking in the melting snow and the shoots are starting deep within the earth. This is also St. Bridget's Day that is celebrated by the Celtic and French; also known as St. Blaize, who is the Goddess that holds water sacred. Blessings of bodies of water are traditionally done at this time. Imbolc is the term for "ewe's milk," and this is the time when the lambs are giving birth and the ewe's produce milk for their young.

God – The God is a young Boy during this celebration.

Goddess – The Goddess is in the Mother aspect who still cares for and looks after the young Boy God.

Colors – Any colors you see in nature can be used at this time, such as white, brown, green, silver, and gold.

Altar – A lot of candles, seeds for the upcoming planting season, drawings of your upcoming garden and pictures of your gardens from previous years. You can also put flowers and a Sun wheel on your altar.

Activities – Here is a small list of things that can be done to celebrate this joyous day. I encourage you to look for more things to add to this list.

- Watch the Sun rise and set
- Plan out garden for the spring and summer
- Organize and order seeds for garden
- Make rain sticks
- Create a Sun wheel wreath
- Relax by a bonfire
- Make bees wax candles
- Create candles using recycled wax from old candles
- Plan your outside circle construction
- Collect stones and paint symbols that are sacred to you on them
- Cover pinecones and oranges with peanut butter and roll them in seeds for the birds, to be set outside
- Perform divination:
  - Reading auras

- o Tarot cards
- o Oracle cards
- o Scrying
- o Rune readings
- o IChing
- o Astrology
- o Automatic writing
- o Dream interpretation
- o Read tea leaves or coffee grounds
- Blessing of your garden using dried herbs, cornmeal and salt
- Self-dedication rituals
- Have family members sit in a circle and take turns narrating guided meditations to visit animals that are still in hibernation

Incense

This is a very versatile recipe, use the amounts of each ingredient that you are called to use. Combine all ingredients into a glass container and burn on a charcoal block or in a bonfire during the celebration of the Candlemas season.

- Dried rosemary
- Dried basil
- Dried peppermint
- Dried sage

YouTube at the following link:
http://www.youtube.com/watch?v=W08Bv_lNowg

Oil

In a ½ oz. clean glass bottle, fill up to the shoulder with jojoba or other carrier oil. Add the following essential oils and ingredients to the bottle.

- 3 drops basil essential oil
- 3 drops peppermint essential oil
- 3 drops rosemary essential oil
- 1 small piece of dried sage
- 1 citrine chip

YouTube at the following link:
http://www.youtube.com/watch?v=W08Bv_lNowg

Traditional French Honey Cake

There is nothing better than smelling a freshly baked cake in your home during this time of year. This is a fantastic traditional honey cake that is quick and easy and is perfect for the little ones to help out with. You can prepare this the night before and have it ready to go for your celebration.

Ingredients:
- 2 ½ cups flour
- ½ tsp baking soda
- 2 ½ tsp baking powder
- 1 heaping tsp coriander
- 1 heaping tsp allspice
- 1 tsp cinnamon
- 1 tsp ginger

- 4 eggs beaten or 12 Tbs flax egg substitute (see recipe on page 126)
- 1 ¼ cup sugar
- ½ cup oil
- 1 cup honey or agave nectar

Preheat oven to 350°F. Grease and flour a round baking dish, set aside. Combine all ingredients until mixed well. Pour into pan and bake 40 – 50 minutes depending on altitude and type of pan used, check after 40 minutes. Can be served with frosting, but is traditionally served plain.

YouTube video at the following link:
http://www.youtube.com/watch?v=EuADBfi0k5A

Rain Sticks

On this season of Candlemas, we begin to look for the signs of spring. These rain sticks symbolize the spring rains that will soon come to wash away the gloom of winter. Using the rain sticks outside will help to welcome in the spring and all the new life that is germinating under the frozen land that will soon come forth. This is a fun craft for people of all ages.

Items needed:
- 1 mailing tube
- 1 pound of nails that are the same length as the diameter of the mailing tube
- 1 to 2 cups of rice
- Duct tape
- Hammer

Pound all of the nails into the mailing tube using a hammer. Tape one end of the mailing tube so that it is secure. Open the other end of the tube and pour in the desired amount of rice, this is what creates the rain sound effect. Once you have the desired amount of rice and have achieved your desired sound, tape that end securely with the tape. To complete, wrap the entire tube in a spiral fashion using the duct tape to secure nails in place.

YouTube at the following link:
http://www.youtube.com/watch?v=Poy81oNgawU

Solar Wheel Wreath

This ancient symbol has been used in spiritual rites to represent the balance in everything and, in this case, to remind us of the Sun's growing strength every day.

Items needed:
- ☉ 1 plain wreath
- ☉ Yellow cloth ribbon

Wrap the wreath with the ribbon to form a solar cross, hang on front door to welcome in the spring.

Candlemas Sabbat – Full Ritual

Items for ritual:

- ☉ Large clear bowl filled with water

- ๑ Floating white candles (enough for everyone in the circle)
- ๑ Cauldron with tea light in it
- ๑ Rosemary and bay leaves
- ๑ One seven day white candle
- ๑ Usual ritual items

Insert into ritual circle format

Ring bell:

"Behold the season of Candlemas. The depth of winter is upon us and the Earth is still covered in a blanket of snow. The Sun grows stronger and stronger with each passing day. The seeds below shall soon begin to sprout and creatures, big and small will start to bear young for this is the cycle of death and rebirth."

Take the rosemary and bay leaf and hold them in your hand, focusing on the new life that is germinating under the ground in every seed. Light tea light in mini cauldron and ring bell three times. Sprinkle crushed herbs onto the flame and say:

"As the days grow longer, spring is upon us, let us smell the refreshing scent of rosemary and bay. May the cobwebs of the past year be brushed away."

Ring bell once:

"The Goddess is awakening below the surface, seeds are germinating and animal's bellies are growing with little ones in their womb. The God is growing stronger with each passing day and feels the yearning begin for the fertility cycle that is upon us."

Move the Goddess and God statues together in the center of the altar.

Light seven day candle:

"We honor you, Mother Gaia, most blessed one. As this candle burns through this night we thank you for the renewed life you offer us all. As you emerge from the dark to the light."

Have each person in the circle think about their intention for the upcoming year, then have them light one of the floating candles in the bowl of water.

"Great Goddess with these flames, bless the spark of life that burns within us. Keep us safe and healthy in mind and body throughout the year. Let this light rekindle our passions for our dreams that are deep within us."

Touch the water from the bowl of floating candles, then sprinkle each person with the water as you say:

"Great Goddess Brigit, whose sacred well is eternal, bless this water with your essence. Bless our mind, let our imaginations pull from your well and flow with clarity. Bless our hearts, may our passion and love speak through us. Bless our hands, may our crafts be skillful. May our work find those who will honor and treasure it. Blessed be."

[Finish ritual with the format chosen from chapter 2]

~ Notes ~

~ *N*otes ~

Chapter 5

Ostara

Time – N.H ~ When the Sun is in 1 degree of Aries – March 20 – 23 / S.H. ~ When the Sun is in 1 degree of Libra – September 21 – 23.

Meaning of the Season – This is the time of the Spring Equinox, when the light and dark (day and night) are in balance. Ostara symbolizes the fertility of the Earth. Lilies are a symbol of the season and are given to men and woman who are courting. Eggs are given as a symbol of rebirth and a fresh start in life and in the year.

God – The God is young and playful at this time, akin to Krishna, very jovial and a trickster.

Goddess – The Goddess is now the Maiden Goddess of spring. The tale of Demeter and Persephone is a traditional tale that is told at this time. This tale tells about Persephone, the daughter of Demeter, and how she goes into the underworld to satisfy her need for adventure and curiosity, and ends up staying longer than she anticipated. Her mother, Demeter, mourns her daughter's absence until one day she finally returns. I encourage you to go seek out the full story and make this part of your Sabbat tradition.

Colors – Any colors you see in nature can be used at this time, such as pink, blue, purple, green, and yellow.

Altar – The altar arrangement should be fresh and simple, with small statues of rabbits, plenty of eggs and lots of flowers.

Activities – Here is a small list of things that can be done to celebrate this joyous day. I encourage you to look for more things to add to this list.

- Watch the Sun rise and set
- Wreath making
- Color eggs
- Decorate trees outside with plastic eggs
- Retell the tale of Demeter and Persephone
- Retell the tale of the rabbit who offers eggs to the Goddess
- Bless seeds for the garden
- Begin to germinate seeds in pots
- Examine the balance in your life

- Stirring's meditation – YouTube video at the following link: http://www.youtube.com/watch?v=T5UxSQUEs98
- Connect with the Fairies or Divas on your land
- Make egg shakers
- Have a springtime treasure hunt
- Dance in your yard to awaken the energy of the land

Incense

This is a very versatile recipe, use the amounts of each ingredient that you are called to use. Combine all ingredients into a glass container and burn on a charcoal block or in a bonfire during the celebration of the Ostara season.

- Sandalwood
- Dried jasmine flowers
- Dried rose petals

YouTube video at the following link:
http://www.youtube.com/watch?v=CKML9xxempc

Oil

In a ½ oz. clean glass bottle, fill up to the shoulder with jojoba or other carrier oil. Add the following essential oils and ingredients to the bottle.

- 1 drop of sandalwood essential oil
- 3 drops of rose absolute essential oil
- 3 drops of jasmine absolute essential oil

๏ 1 citrine chip

YouTube video at the following link:
http://www.youtube.com/watch?v=CKML9xxempc

Hot Cross Buns

This traditional recipe is a favorite for this Sabbat. This bread, marked with a + on the top, symbolizes the Sun wheel and the balance of all of life at this time. There are hundreds of variations of this recipe, so feel free to modify the asterisked* items for things of your own liking.

Also note that there are two versions of this recipe, an overnight version and a same day version. Please be aware of this before you begin this recipe.

Ingredients for fruit mixture:
๏ 1/3 cup dried fruits * (cherries, cranberries, raisins, dried apple slices, apricot's or other)
๏ ½ cup orange juice* warmed (can also use any type of Spirits such as bourbon)
๏ Zest from 1 lemon or 1 orange

Ingredients for dough:
๏ 1 cup milk (soy, goat, almond etc.)
๏ 2 Tbs yeast
๏ ½ cup sugar
๏ 2 tsp salt
๏ 1/3 cup butter or butter substitute at room temperature
๏ 2 tsp cinnamon

- ⓢ 1 tsp nutmeg
- ⓢ 4 eggs or 12Tbs flax egg substitute (see recipe on page 73)
- ⓢ 5 cups flour

Brush on before baking:
- ⓢ 1 egg white (optional)

Ingredients for icing:
- ⓢ 1 1/3 cups powdered sugar
- ⓢ Zest from one lemon
- ⓢ Juice from 1 lemon or 1 orange

Candy or cooking thermometer

Put dried fruits into small glass dish, pour warm orange juice over the fruits and set aside.

In a small sauce pan, warm milk or milk substitute to between 100 to 110°F. In a large glass bowl pour warmed milk into the bottom and sprinkle yeast over the top. Gently stir until it is dissolved.

In the same bowl add and blend together to the yeast milk mixture, the sugar, salt, butter, cinnamon, nutmeg and eggs. Gradually add 1 cup of flour at a time. When all the flour is added, the dough should still feel slightly sticky. Cover and let the dough rest for 30 – 45 minutes.

Take dough out of bowl and place on floured surface. Wash bowl and butter it, then set aside. Pour off liquid from the bowl of dried fruits; begin adding the soaked fruits and zest to the dough. Knead the dough until it is very elastic; it should remain slightly sticky; using too much flour in this process will make the buns tough. Once the dough is elastic, place it in the prepared bowl, cover with plastic wrap and let rise overnight in the refrigerator.

Note: By having the dough rise overnight, you allow all of the flavors to nicely incorporate with the bread itself. If you do not want to wait, then:

> Cover the bowl with a towel and place in a warm area until dough doubles, punch down and proceed with the recipe.

The next morning take the dough out of the refrigerator and let sit for about 45 minutes on the counter still covered. After 45 min punch once and proceed.

Grease a large baking pan with butter or oil, set aside. Divide dough into 24 equal pieces and shape into balls. Place dough balls onto baking sheet about ½ inch apart. Cover with a clean dish towel and let rise in a warm area, until doubled. This will usually take about 1 ½ hours.

Preheat oven to 400°F.

After buns have risen, take a sharp knife and cut an equal armed cross or + on the top of each bun. Brush them with the egg white and place in center rack of oven.

Bake for 10 minutes, and then reduce the oven temperature to 350°F for about 15 minutes. When the buns are golden brown, they are done. Remove buns from oven and transfer from the hot pan to a cooling rack.

In a small bowl, whisk together the powdered sugar, zest and juice until smooth. Brush on the buns and enjoy warm.

Flax Eggs or Egg Substitute -

This is a wonderful substitute for eggs, if you are vegan or if you are simply out of eggs. They even have a slimy consistency of eggs, though I would not recommend scrambling them.

- ৯ 1/3 cup milled flax seed
- ৯ 1 cup water

Mix thoroughly in a bowl and let sit. Once the mixture reaches egg like consistency, it is ready to use.

3 Tbs = 1 whole egg
Makes enough for six eggs

Egg Shakers

These fun and easy shakers can be used not only for this Sabbat but for any celebration throughout the year. It's simple and quick.

Items needed:

- Markers
- Grains such as lentils or rice
- Plastic eggs – can be found at local grocery stores
- Colorful duct tape
- Scissors

Start by filling up a small bowl with the grains such as lentils or rice, set aside. Then cut one four inch strip of duct tape for each egg shaker you will make; set aside. Open the plastic egg, while holding both sides dip the egg into the grain bowl filling the egg to your desired fullness. Snap the egg shut, seal with duct tape and color with markers. Yay!!!

Ostara Sabbat – Full Ritual

Items for ritual:

- Mini egg candles purple, green and pink (these can be found at most big named retail stores around this time of year)
- Flowers from the yard (or store)
- A pot with soil
- Seed of Intention – this can be any seed that is alive and can germinate (not roasted or cooked)
- Small vessel of water
- Layout of new garden
- List of new garden plants
- Usual ritual items

Inserted into ritual circle format

Ring bell:

"Behold the season of Ostara, when all the Earth bursts forth with life. The fragrance of flowers is sweet in the air. Life renews itself with your mysteries great Goddess. The God grows eager in his youth, and is bursting with the promise of summer."

Light egg candles:

Sprinkle the flowers around the inside perimeter of the sacred circle as you say:

"Goddess and God frolic and play; stir up the creatures along your way."

Ring bell:

Hold up the pot of soil and say:

"Goddess bless this soil with your fertility and vitality. Prepare this soil for our seeds of intention. May they find nutrients in your cauldron of rebirth."

Pick up the vessel of water and bless it by saying:

"Goddess Brigit, bless this water so that it may stir the life inside this seed."

Hold your seed in your hands and focus on your intention of what you want to manifest in the coming year.

"Oh Goddess Ostara, bless this seed with fertility that life may spark in the depths of your womb."

As you put the seed into the soil, say what comes into your heart. Pour a small amount of water onto the seed. (When the seed has sprouted, transplant it into the earth someplace suitable for it to grow.)

Lay out garden plan that includes the new plants for the next growing season.

"Goddess and God, let this garden be blessed by your sunlight, rains, cool breezes and refreshing evenings. Let it be fertile to receive our seeds and transplants that have been prepared for your soil, so they may grow and ripen, heavy with your bounty. Know that all who will partake of this bounty will forever honor the feast that springs forth from your womb."

Ring bell three times.

[Finish ritual with the format chosen from chapter 2]

~ Notes ~

~ Notes ~

Chapter 6

Beltane

Time – N.H. ~ When the Sun is in 15 degrees of Taurus – April 30 - May 1 / S.H. ~ When the Sun is in 15 degrees of Scorpio – October 31.

Meaning of the Season – This season is all about fertility, sex, passion, and getting in touch with our primal energies. This is a perfect time to talk about sexuality and healthy sexual relationships with young family members.

God – The God is in the older Boy aspect ready to fertilize the land. He is also referred as the Greenman during this time.

Goddess – The Goddess is a young Maiden ready to welcome the God in the fertility rights known to all beings at this time.

Colors – Any colors you see in nature can be used at this time, such as red, white, green and pastels.

Altar – The altar is simple and elegant with a Maiden Goddess figure and a young God figure. Simple flowers of pastel colors such as a rose, peony or tulip are perfect for this day.

Activities – Here is a small list of things that can be done to celebrate this joyous day. I encourage you to look for more things to add to this list.

- Watch the Sun rise and set
- Jump over a bale fire or bonfire
- Lovers can hold hands and jump over the fire
- Light one candle or a flameless candle and have children jump over it to make wishes
- The Great Rite – Symbolic with Chalice and Athame
- "I Love Me" spell
- Find your animal totem – YouTube video at the following link:
  http://www.youtube.com/watch?v=I3ppUi06y3Y
- Create fairy houses for your home
- Create and dance the May pole
- Discuss sex and sexuality with young family members
- Set out crystals for the fairies in your yard
- Blessings for Mothers
- Blessings for Children
- Give flowers to your loved ones
- Go on nature walks and see what kinds of animals are out and about
- Bring flowers to a local nursing home

- Go to a local zoo to see the newborn animals
- Set out food for wild animals in a local park or in your backyard

Incense

This is a very versatile recipe, use the amounts of each ingredient that you are called to use. Combine all ingredients into a glass container and burn on a charcoal block or in a bonfire during the celebration of the Beltane season.

- Dried rosemary
- Dried catnip
- Dried lavender flowers
- Granular benzoin resin

YouTube Video at the following link:
http://www.youtube.com/watch?v=4t_o48BYHe4

Oil

In a ½ oz. clean glass bottle, fill up to the shoulder with jojoba or other carrier oil. Add the following essential oils and ingredients to the bottle.

- 2 drops rosewood essential oil
- 2 drops rosemary essential oil
- 2 drops geranium essential oil
- 2 drops rose absolute essential oil
- 1 citrine stone

YouTube Video at the following link:
http://www.youtube.com/watch?v=4t_o48BYHe4

Quick Fruit Tarts

Tarts have been around for centuries. Tarts can be sweet or savory and range in size from small to very large. This is a recipe for mini sweet tarts which makes the perfect snack for a potluck or to have around the house during this celebration.

Items needed:
- Mini muffin tin
- Dough round cutter (the top of a glass will do)
- Tart press
- Dough roller
- Spoon

Ingredients:
- One box of ready-made pie crust
- Fruit filling – such as cherry or blueberry
- Fresh fruit cut into small chunks
- Fresh berries

Preheat oven to 450°F. Bring the crust to room temperature and roll out onto cutting board. Press dough round cutter or top of glass into dough to create a dough round for the crust of the tart. Place the dough round into the mini muffin tin and push down on the dough gently, with the tart press, using a rocking motion. Fill the crusts ¾ full with fruit filling or fruit chunks.

Bake for 13 - 15 minutes or until the edges of the tarts are golden brown. Sprinkle with powdered sugar.

YouTube Video at the following link:
http://www.youtube.com/watch?v=hQzG_OGgauE

Ribbon Wind Catchers or Wind Socks

This stunning wind catcher, once completed is perfect for indoor or outdoor use. With each ribbon you can attach a spell or prayer to it while you are making it, creating a powerful magical tool.

Items needed:
- Sewing or embroidery hoop separated
- Tacky glue
- Scissors
- Lots of cloth ribbon
- Four clamps (clothes pins, paper clips etc.)

Separate the embroidery hoop from itself so the inner and outer rings are apart. Take a piece of ribbon and loop it through the inner hoop, bring the ribbon along itself to mimic what it will look like once it is finished. This is to get a visual measurement so you can determine how long you want the ribbon to hang down from the top of the wind catcher. Make sure you have the ribbon looped over the top so that it is folded over. Once you have your length in mind, cut this ribbon; this will be your measuring guide during the first portion of the craft.

Then cut lengths of ribbon based on the piece you previously measured. These ribbons will be twice as long as you want them to be, but when you glue them in place they will be the correct length. Continue to cut ribbon pieces until you have enough ribbon to completely surround the hoop.

Firmly hold the inner ring with one hand and feed the ribbon in with the other to the mid-way point of the ribbon. Transfer the ribbon to the hand that is holding the hoop, to keep it in place, and place a bead of glue on the area of the hoop where the ribbon and hoop meet, press the ribbon onto the glue bead. Continue this process until the entire hoop is covered with ribbon. Set aside to dry. If you are working with children, you can have them complete this process by tying, instead of gluing, the ribbons to the inner ring.

While the inner ring of ribbons is drying, find four long ribbons to use as the hanger and one to use as the ornamentation for the top outside hoop. Take the outer ring and mark four equally spaced places on the ring. Place a thin layer of glue the same width as the ribbon on the outside and inside of the hoop. Then wrap one end of ribbon, starting on the inside edge from underneath, around the hoop so that the ribbon finishes in an upward fashion, clamp in place to dry. This will create one of the four ribbons that will act as a hanger for the wind catcher. Repeat this process three more times having the ribbons equally spaced out around the hoop.

After the outer ring has dried, take your final piece of ribbon and measure the circumference around the hoop and cut to fit. Place a long bead of glue along the entire circumference of the hoop leaving space for the tightening rod. Place the ribbon over the glue and set aside to dry.

Once the completed inner and outer rings have dried completely loosen the tightening rod and place the outer ring over the inner ring and tighten the tightening rod.

Take the four long pieces of ribbon that are attached to the outer hoop and hold them above the hoop and tie the ends together forming a loop at the top. This is how you will hang your wind catcher.

[Author's note: I recommend you watch the YouTube video before attempting this craft as the details are very intricate. I want to make sure you fully understand the directions before trying this out, as cloth ribbon can be a bit pricey.]

YouTube Video at the following link:
http://www.youtube.com/watch?v=PfdGQXd7QiA

Beltane Sabbat – Full Ritual

Items for ritual:

- Dark green candle
- Small vase of flowers from yard
- Adam and Eve root and a small box (found online)
- Mini May pole
- Goblet of wine or juice
- Usual ritual items

Insert into ritual circle format

"Behold the season of Beltane, the day of the joyous union between the Goddess and God."

Move the Goddess and God statues together to the center of the altar. Take the Adam and Eve root and join them together as a symbol of the Goddess and God joining in the fertility rites of Beltane. Place the joined root into a small ornamental box to keep on the altar for this season. (Explain to all in the circle what this symbolizes if you choose or you can remain quiet.)

"Fruitful is the land and all the seas, fruitful as the busy bees."

Raise the goblet with wine or juice and say:

"All hail the great union of the Goddess and God. May their union this night create a great bounty for *all* the world to enjoy."

Pour a libation, take a sip and put it back on altar.

Bale fire – light candle and place on the floor…circle around it as you think of a wish…jump over it as you say your wish.

Mini May Pole – everyone grab a ribbon and go over and under as you sing a traditional song. These songs can be found online.

[Finish ritual with the format chosen from chapter 2]

~ Notes ~

~ Notes ~

Chapter 7

Summer Solstice ~ Litha

Time – N.H. ~ When the Sun is in 1 degree of Cancer – June 21 – 23 / S.H. ~ When the Sun is in 1 degree of Capricorn – December 21 – 23.

Meaning of the Season – This is the time of the longest day and shortest night of the year. The land is full and lush with food, grains, berries vegetables and flowers. All of life is beaming at this time.

God – The God is in the Father aspect of self and is represented as the Holly King. The Holly King and the Oak

King have a duel on this day to determine who will rule over the next half of the year.

Goddess – The Goddess is pregnant with the bounty of the earth. Her aspect is the Mother Gaia.

Colors – Any colors you see in nature can be used at this time, such as yellow, orange, green, purple and red.

Altar – The altar should be adorned with lots of local flowers, bright colors, a Goddess and God representation, sunflowers and all things that symbolize the height of the summer season.

Activities – Here is a small list of things that can be done to celebrate this joyous day. I encourage you to look for more things to add to this list.

- Watch the Sun rise and set
- Blessings for Fathers
- Go for walks
- Collect items from nature ie.. pinecones, leaves, stones, etc.
- Harvest herbs at high noon on the Solstice
- Create herbal smudge bundles
- Save the stocks and stems from harvested herbs for a wicker man
- Create a wicker man
- Bale fire or bonfire
- Give offerings for the Fairies outside your home, such as sweets and crystals

- Create a herbal blend for home protection
- Craft cinnamon bundles for protection
- Tie ribbons in trees for Air spells
- Seek out a local nature preserve to explore
- Create a wreath out of local flowers and bless them and put it into a local water way
- Make a pair of maracas
- Buy a small bird house at a local crafting store and paint it to create a fairy house
- Create a God's eye or evil eye – YouTube video at the following link: http://www.youtube.com/watch?v=MyWsASgeRKY&feature=related
- Rededication of service to the Goddess
- Have a picnic at a local park
- Create a dream pillow filled with lavender and rosemary

Incense

This is a very versatile recipe, use the amounts of each ingredient that you are called to use. Combine all ingredients into a glass container and burn on a charcoal block or in a bonfire during the celebration of the Summer Solstice season.

- Dried peppermint leaves
- Red sandalwood powder
- Copal resin

YouTube video at the following link:
http://www.youtube.com/watch?v=Hzyix2UCf8Q

Oil

In a ½ oz. clean glass bottle, fill up to the shoulder with jojoba or other carrier oil. Add the following essential oils and ingredients to the bottle.

- ๑ 2 drops peppermint essential oil
- ๑ 3 drops sweet orange or orange essential oil
- ๑ 3 drops ginger essential oil
- ๑ 1 citrine chip

YouTube video at the following link:
http://www.youtube.com/watch?v=Hzyix2UCf8Q

Light and Easy Lemon Cake

This is a favorite traditional recipe for my family to make in the spring time. It's fast and easy and the kids love to drizzle on the frosting at the end.

Ingredients for cake:
- ๑ 2 cups flour
- ๑ ½ cup sugar
- ๑ Finely grated zest from 2 lemons
- ๑ 3 eggs beaten or 9 Tbs flax egg substitute (recipe on page 126)
- ๑ ½ cup milk or milk substitute
- ๑ ½ cup vegetable oil
- ๑ Thin lemon wedges for garnishment

Ingredients for frosting:
- ๑ 1 cup powdered sugar (more or less if need be)
- ๑ Juice from 2 lemons

Preheat oven to 350°F. Using spray oil, grease an 8 or 9 inch round pan, dust with flour and set aside. Mix together flour, sugar and lemon zest. In a small bowl, whisk together eggs, milk and oil. Fold gently into the bowl of dry ingredients.

Pour into prepared pan. Bake for 35 - 40 minutes until done. Let cake sit for about 5 minutes then turn out onto a wire rack so it can cool completely.

While cake is cooking combine powdered sugar and lemon juice in a small bowl until smooth. When cake is done, drizzle over the top and serve.

Cinnamon Bundles for Protection

Cinnamon is a bark which has highly protective properties and can be used in this craft with confidence knowing that wherever this bundle resides will surely be protected. These bundles are perfect for your home, office, vehicles or any space you would like to protect.

Items needed:
- ๑ Three cinnamon sticks
- ๑ Cloth ribbon of your choice

Tie cinnamon sticks together at the midway point, looping the ribbon around each stick to create a tight bundle. Leave enough ribbon on the ends to create a long loop so you can hang the bundle up. Once the sticks are all tightly bound together, bring the remaining ribbon together towards one end and tie to create a loop that will be used for hanging the cinnamon stick bundle.

YouTube video at the following link:
http://www.youtube.com/watch?v=hILgyAjZZYg

Spell Stars

A traditional recipe used to create Yule ornaments, one year while making them, my family decided to put a twist on the tradition. We decided to create "Spell Stars." While making these stars, or whatever shape you decide, think about what you will be using them for. Infuse them with that energy while you are making them. Not only can these be for spells, they can be used for protective amulets for a backpack, vehicle, home or office. The sky is the limit. Yay!!!

Items needed:
- Applesauce
- Ground cinnamon
- Cookie cutter in the shape of a star
- Rolling pin
- Cutting board

Combine about ½ cup applesauce and ¾ cup of cinnamon into a bowl and mix thoroughly. Keep adding cinnamon until the mixture is a doughy consistency.

Roll dough until it is about ¼ inch thick and use your cookie cutter to cut out the shape. Place shape on a cookie cooling rack or paper towel. Turn shapes daily until they are completely dry.

YouTube video at the following link:
http://www.youtube.com/watch?v=0GFJw1gPibM

Summer Solstice Sabbat – Full Ritual

Items for ritual:

- Cornmeal and protection herbal blend to sprinkle around the perimeter of your property
- Cinnamon sticks and pinecones
- Wicker man with numerous loose ribbons (enough for two or three ribbons for each person in attendance)
- Cauldron of rain water
- Holly King and Oak King representations and candles
- Usual ritual items

Insert into ritual circle format

Ring bell:

"Behold the season of high summer and the Summer Solstice. We celebrate as joy and happiness flows within all on this day. The Sun God is at his peak in the sky. The Goddess is heavy with pregnancy. Today we celebrate the light, for tomorrow the light will begin to wane and sink deeper and deeper into the night."

"The Oak King who has grown old guarding over the land since Winter Solstice, does not want to give up his guardianship over this realm. The Oak King and Holly King do battle."

Do a mock battle between the two kings:

"The Oak King has lost this battle and retreats to the other realm where he will await for the Winter Solstice, a time when he is at the height of his strength. Farewell old Oak King, until next Solstice, we bid you farewell."

Extinguish God candle and take the Oak King representation and candle off altar and replace it with the Holly King representation and candle.

Ring God bell once:

"We welcome the Holly King, who comes to us in the brightest of days on this Summer Solstice. Through this mystery of death and rebirth, we are reminded of the promise of nature, that which is born will surely be born again from the womb of the Goddess. We welcome the waning year through the beginning of the dying season. All hail the God tonight!"

Place hands over cornmeal, herbs, cinnamon and pinecones:

"I call upon all the elements and the Goddess and God to come and infuse these items with your blessings and enhance their essence so that when they are dispersed across this land they protect it with your mighty power."

Set down herbs; pick up the cauldron of water and say:

"Oh great Goddess bless this water tonight, Oh Yemaya, powerful protectress, bathe us with your glory as we rededicate ourselves to being in your service."

Take the cauldron of rain water and rededicate all in the circle who wish it so. Put some water on their feet, heart, eye area, and the crown of the head and say:

"Bless our feet as we walk where you guide us. Bless our heart as we love as you have loved us. Bless our eyes so we can see others as you see us. Bless our crowns so our divine connection to you will be ever present in our lives."

"As we stand here cleansed by your waters, please allow your grace to flow through us in our actions and words while acting as your ambassadors. Bless all who are present in this circle and all who come in contact with us, so that they may see your glory shine through us and strive to feel that love and grace in their lives. Blessed Be."

With a completed wicker man in the circle, distribute ribbons for all who want to participate. Have everyone think of something they are finished with and infuse that energy into the ribbon. Tie the ribbons on the wicker man, for each item to be banished, and burn it in the bale fire.

[Finish ritual with the format chosen from chapter 2]

~ Notes ~

~ Notes ~

~ *Notes* ~

Chapter 8

Lammas

Time – N.H ~ When the Sun is in 15 degrees of Leo – August 1 / S.H. ~ When the Sun is in 15 degrees of Aquarius – February 2.

Meaning of the Season – This is the celebration of the first harvest. Other traditional celebrations include the English celebration which is called Loafmass, the Irish festival honoring Lugh, and the Roman festival honoring Mercury.

God – The God is in the Sage, grandfather, or wise aspect during this time.

Goddess – The Goddess is in the Mother aspect during this time of the year.

Colors – Any colors you see in nature can be used at this time, such as green, yellow, red, and orange.

Altar – The altar should have an abundance of fruits and vegetables at this time, a Goddess and God representation as well as a baked good created from the harvested crops.

Activities – Here is a small list of things that can be done to celebrate this joyous day. I encourage you to look for more things to add to this list.

- Watch the Sun rise and set
- Make tea from herbs grown in your yard (rosemary is very good)
- Make corn dollies
- Honor the teachers in your life
- Harvest vegetables and herbs
- Go berry picking
- Create herbal smudge bundles
- Make offering stones
- Bake wheat bread
- Bake cobblers and fruit desserts
- Bless and donate food to a food bank
- Have a bonfire and burn old corn dollies
- Go star gazing
- Volunteer at a local soup kitchen
- Go for a walk in nature to talk about how the changing of the seasons is occurring
- Make drums out of old containers, such as plastic buckets or oat containers

- ๑ Gather together drums and have a drum circle with friends

Incense

This is a very versatile recipe, use the amounts of each ingredient that you are called to use. Combine all ingredients into a glass container and burn on a charcoal block or in a bonfire during the celebration of the Lammas season.

- ๑ Dried sandalwood
- ๑ Dried patchouli leaf
- ๑ Dried rosemary

YouTube video at the following link:
http://www.youtube.com/watch?v=p39UR2RGJQw

Oil

In a ½ oz. clean glass bottle, fill up to the shoulder with jojoba or other carrier oil. Add the following essential oils and ingredients to the bottle.

- ๑ 1 small piece of blonde sandalwood
- ๑ 2 drops of patchouli essential oil
- ๑ 1 drop of rosemary essential oil
- ๑ 1 citrine chip

YouTube video at the following link:
http://www.youtube.com/watch?v=p39UR2RGJQw

Blackberry Cornmeal Muffins

With the ripening of the land, heavy and abundant, this recipe
uses what is plentifully and ripe. Use fresh (or frozen)
blackberries to create a special treat found inside of a traditional
cornmeal muffin.

Ingredients:
- 1 ¼ cup flour
- ¾ cup cornmeal
- ¼ cup sugar
- ½ tsp salt
- 2 tsp baking powder

- 1 cup milk or milk replacement (soy, goat, or almond)
- ¼ cup oil
- 1 egg or 3Tbs flax egg substitute
- Small amount of honey or agave nectar - enough to
  make your sacred symbol on the top of the batter
- Blackberry jam – or fresh/frozen blackberries

Take out jam and warm to room temperature. Preheat oven to
350°F. Grease muffin tins with oil and set aside.

Combine dry ingredients; flour, cornmeal, sugar, salt and baking
powder and mix well. Then add the milk, oil and egg or egg
replacement. If the batter is dry add a splash more milk.
Add a small amount of honey or agave nectar.

Fill the prepared muffin tins ½ to ¾ of the way full. Put one
spoonful of jam on the top of each filled muffin cup.

Bake for 20 - 25 minutes until done.

YouTube video at the following link:
http://www.youtube.com/watch?v=exi9svpS5tk

Flax Eggs or Egg Substitute

This is a wonderful substitute for eggs, if you are vegan or if you are simply out of eggs. They even have a slimy consistency of eggs, though I would not recommend scrambling them.

- 1/3 cup milled flax seed
- 1 cup water

Mix thoroughly in a bowl and let sit. Once the mixture reaches egg like consistency, it is ready to use.

3 Tbs = 1 whole egg
Makes enough for six eggs

Corn Dollies

Corn dollies have been used for centuries as a child's toy and in spiritual symbolism of the abundance of the land. This is a very quick technique for an eclectic looking corn dolly.

Items needed:
- Ribbon
- Scissors
- Corn husks – found in the produce section of a grocery store, or from freshly shucked corn

ⓢ Markers

First take three corn husks and put them together with the narrow tips together. Fold down the narrow tops of the husks, about 1 ½ inches down, to make the heads of the dolly. Fold in the sides of the husk slightly. Take a ribbon and tie it about 1 to 2 inches down from the fold, tight around the corn husk, this will make the head. Next take a marker and make the face of the corn dolly. Then take the scissors and cut diagonally into the body portion of the dolly to make arms.

YouTube video at the following link:
http://www.youtube.com/watch?v=zaTDdGYP84w

Lammas Sabbat – Full Ritual

Items for ritual:

ⓢ Seasonal vegetables that will be used for the meal
ⓢ Yellow candle
ⓢ Small vase of flowers from yard
ⓢ Cornmeal for the meal as well as the house blessing
ⓢ Usual ritual items
ⓢ Wheat bread
ⓢ Blackberry cobbler and drink for the cake/wine part of ritual

Insert into ritual circle format

Ring bell:

"Behold the season of Lammas, the first harvest. We celebrate the marvelous and heavy bounty the Goddess has given to all creatures of the land."

Hold hands with everyone in the circle and say:

"As we dance and spiral, we celebrate these gifts and honor the womb of the Goddess from which we all have come from."

Have two people drop one hand from each other, to create a gap. Have one person be the start and the other is the ending of the dance line. The person acting as the beginning, start to dance in a spiral until everyone is close and cannot move. Then have the end become the beginning and spiral out to form a circle again.

Ring bell:

Hold hands over bread:

"Goddess and God, thank you for this bread, a symbol of your joint fertility. We bless and break this bread in your honor."

Tear a piece off and put into the libation bowl or on the ground. Save the rest for evening meal.

"Thank you for the sustenance you continually provide, we are ever grateful."

Light yellow candle:

Hold hands over the cornmeal and veggies from yard that will be used to make the meal for the evening:

"Goddess and God, infuse this cornmeal with your blessings and protection, that it may encircle those who love you. Bless these vegetables and as we eat them let us remember the bountiful blessings you have given to us this year so far. So Must It Be."

[Finish ritual with the format chosen from chapter 2]

~ Notes ~

~ *N*otes ~

Chapter 9

Mabon

Time – N.H. ~ When the Sun is in 1 degree of Libra – Sept 21 – 23 / S.H. ~ When the Sun is in 1 degree of Aries – March 21 – 23.

Meaning of the Season – This is the time of the fall Equinox, when the balance of light and dark, night and day occur. This is also the second harvest and is sometimes known as the "Witches Thanksgiving." This Sabbat is named after Mabon, a Welsh God, who is the counterbalance of Persephone in springtime.

God – The God is known at this time as the horned one or the God of the wild beasts; he rules over any creature that lives in the wild or in captivity.

Goddess – The Goddess is in the Crone, grandmother, or wise aspect also known as the Goddess Cerridwen.

God and Goddess - QuanYin who has been known throughout history as both male and female, in many different cultures, is another wonderful way to bring in balance on this day. Use this deity on your altar to represent the balance of masculine and feminine in each of us.

Colors – Any colors you see in nature can be used at this time, such as orange, red, brown, green, and yellow.

Altar – Gifts from loved ones are a wonderful addition to this season's altar. Nonperishable items that will go to a food bank, seasonal fruits and vegetables from the harvest, as well as baked goods also go well on this altar.

Activities – Here is a small list of things that can be done to celebrate this joyous day. I encourage you to look for more things to add to this list.

- Watch the Sun rise and set
- Go to an orchard and pick apples
- Make applesauce
- Give offerings of thanks to ancestors
- Make spell stars
- Make a harvest wreath
- Go to a local waterway and feed the ducks or geese
- Harvest fruits and vegetables from the land
- Visit a farmers market

- Tour a local farm
- Bake Apple Mabon bread
- Make berry jam
- Visit a local zoo and put blessings of health on the animals
- Restoring the balance of self and home
  - Chakra meditations
  - Space clearings

Incense

This is a very versatile recipe, use the amounts of each ingredient that you are called to use. Combine all ingredients into a glass container and burn on a charcoal block or in a bonfire during the celebration of the Mabon season.

- Red sandalwood
- Dried patchouli
- Benzoin granules
- Dried white sage
- Myrrh resin

YouTube video at the following link:
http://www.youtube.com/watch?v=MnY3zrimgoA

Oil

In a ½ oz. clean glass bottle, fill up to the shoulder with jojoba or other carrier oil. Add the following essential oils and ingredients to the bottle.

- 6 drops sage essential oil
- 5 drops patchouli essential oil
- 3 drops myrrh essential oil
- 2 drops rose absolute essential oil
- 1 citrine chip
- 1 small piece of white sage

YouTube video at the following link:
http://www.youtube.com/watch?v=MnY3zrimgoA

Apple Mabon Bread

The season of Mabon is filled with the rich warm scents of apples, spices and the wonderful fall breeze. This traditional apple bread, embraces the essence of the season for everyone to enjoy.

Ingredients:
- 2 ½ cups grated apple
- 2 cups dried fruit (I recommend dried cranberries or cherries)
- 1 ½ cups boiling water
- 3 Tbs olive oil
- 1 cup honey or agave nectar
- 1 ½ tsp cinnamon
- 1 ½ tsp allspice
- 1 ½ tsp salt
- ½ tsp cloves

- 3 cups flour
- 1 ½ tsp baking soda

114

- ꩜ ¾ cup finely chopped nuts

Preheat oven to 350°F. Grease two loaf pans and set aside. Combine first 9 ingredients together in a bowl and set aside.

In another bowl, mix together the last three ingredients. Add the wet mixture to the flour mixture and stir until combined. Pour into prepared loaf pans and bake for one hour.

Let rest on rack until cool. Serve with fresh berry jam.

YouTube video at the following link:
http://www.youtube.com/watch?v=PWiciaxVIlo

Harvest Wreath or Found Item Wreath

My family loves to go on hikes and walks throughout the year. We tend to bring home pockets and handfuls of treasures from each of these walks. By this time each year, we have bowls overflowing with natures treasures. This is the perfect use for natural and found objects.

Items needed:

- ꩜ One grapevine wreath
- ꩜ Found objects such as:
    - o Feathers
    - o Acorns
    - o Pinecones
    - o Leaves
    - o Flowers

- o Holey stones
- o Shells
- o Fossils
- o Dried seed pods
- ๑ Dried fruits rounds from an:
  - o Orange
  - o Apple
  - o Lemon
- ๑ Anything else that calls to you
- ๑ Fishing line
- ๑ Ribbon
- ๑ Scissors
- ๑ Paint
- ๑ Paint brush

Gather all of your items, and if you choose, you can paint some of the items to give them a festive touch before you put them onto the wreath. Attach items to wreath using fishing line. Use as a center piece during Mabon, then hang on door after your celebration.

YouTube video at the following link:
http://www.youtube.com/watch?v=ngO-i_ZW5PU

Mabon Sabbat – Full Ritual

Items for ritual:

- ๑ Brown candle
- ๑ Seasonal flowers

- Apple Mabon bread
- Plate of seasonal food
- Goods for donation
- Bell
- Grape juice
- Familiars
- Treat for the animals
- Usual ritual items

Insert into ritual circle format

Ring bell:

"Behold the season of Mabon, time of the second harvest. As we joyously gather and harvest the bounty from the land, let us give thanks to the Goddess and God. Let us also remember those who do not have enough to eat at this time and be grateful for the bounty we have before us."

"Tonight all things are in balance: feminine and masculine, dark and light, death and rebirth. Tonight the God begins to wane and die. Soon he will pass on to the womb of the Goddess and begin the cycle of life all over again at Yule. The Wheel of the Year turns and we honor this cycle knowing that each turn is normal and found in nature as well as in ourselves."

Touch the goods for donation:

"Goddess and God bless this food and infuse it with your love and prosperity so that all that partake of it feel your presence."

Light the brown candle:

If family pets are available, take them into the circle and hold them gently and say:

"We thank you for sharing your lives with us, and we ask the Goddess and God to bless and surround you with health and safety and be ever at your side."

Give them a special treat.

[Finish ritual with the format chosen from chapter 2]

~ Notes ~

~ Notes ~

Chapter 10

Samhain

Time – N.H ~ When the Sun is in 15 degrees of Scorpio – October 31 / S.H ~ When the Sun is in 15 degrees of Taurus – May 1.

Meaning of the Season – This is the third and final harvest of the year. This is a time to remember those who have passed on before us. We celebrate reincarnation and the cycle of life with our close friends and family members. This is also when some Witches celebrate the Celtic New Year. The veil between the two worlds is at its thinnest and is a great time to contact those who have passed on within the last year.

God – The God has passed on to the other world and has now re-entered the Goddess as an embryo to be born again at Yule.

Goddess – The Goddess is in the Crone or grandmother aspect at this time. She is commonly referred to as the Goddess Cerridwen who is the Goddess that watches over the cauldron of life, death and rebirth. She escorts the souls from this life to Summerland and back again. The Goddess is also known as the Mother Goddess who is pregnant with the God.

Colors – Any colors you see in nature can be used at this time, such as brown, black, orange, and burgundy.

Altar – A traditional altar at this time is adorned with images of skulls to remind us of our own mortality, any items that were from the final harvest from the land, as well as photos of ancestors and candles.

Activities – Here is a small list of things that can be done to celebrate this joyous day. I encourage you to look for more things to add to this list.

- Watch the Sun rise and set
- Harvest fruits and vegetables
- Craft sugar skulls
- Bake sweet skull bread
- Create an ancestor altar
- Make the favorite foods of those who have passed on
- Have a "Dumb Supper"
- Go to a Day of the Dead celebration
- Leave apples out for visiting Spirits
- Put a candle in a window for your ancestors
- Visit the grave sites of those who have passed on

- Tell your favorite stories about the people who have passed on
- Preform divination:
    - Reading auras
    - Tarot cards
    - Oracle cards
    - Scrying – mirror, candle, crystals, water, etc…
    - Rune readings
    - IChing
    - Astrology
    - Automatic writing
    - Dream interpretation
    - Read tea leaves or coffee grounds
    - Use a Pendulum to answer yes or no questions
    - Read and interpret smoke swirls from the bonfire

Incense

This is a very versatile recipe, use the amounts of each ingredient that you are called to use. Combine all ingredients into a glass container and burn on a charcoal block or in a bonfire during the celebration of the Samhain season.

- Dried mullein leaf
- Dried patchouli leaf
- Sandalwood powder
- Dried white sage

YouTube video at the following link:
http://www.youtube.com/watch?v=yUrgKz9Ge6s

Oil

In a ½ oz. clean glass bottle, fill up to the shoulder with jojoba or other carrier oil. Add the following essential oils and ingredients to the bottle.

- 2 drops sage essential oil
- 2 drops patchouli essential oil
- 2 drops sweet orange essential oil
- 1 citrine chip

YouTube video at the following link:
http://www.youtube.com/watch?v=yUrgKz9Ge6s

Sweet Skull Bread

The days are short and the nights are long, with that comes the sultry allure of comfort foods. This is a warm rich bread that will have you nibbling in no time. Using traditional bread methods this is a perfect recipe to create a beautiful presence in your Sabbat celebration; have all who gather together with you participate in the kneading and preparation of this bread.

Ingredients:
- 2 Tbs dry yeast
- ½ cup warm water
- Pinch of sugar
- ½ cup milk or milk substitute
- 6 Tbs flax eggs (or 2 whole eggs)
- ½ cup honey or agave nectar
- ¾ cup pumpkin puree

- 2 tsp ginger
- 2 tsp cinnamon
- 2 tsp nutmeg
- 2 tsp allspice
- 1 tsp sea salt
- 5 to 6 cups of unbleached flour

Preheat oven to 350°F. Grease a large glass bowl and set aside. In a medium glass bowl add the warm water, and then sprinkle in the yeast and sugar. After the yeast mixture foams, add all remaining ingredients except flour. Once the mixture is smooth, add one cup of flour at a time, making sure it is completely incorporated. Once dough is too tough to stir, put onto a flat surface and start kneading the remaining flour in the dough ½ cup at a time. Once dough is springy and resists kneading, form into a ball. Place dough into greased glass bowl, turn, cover and set in warm place until the dough has doubled in size; about 20 - 30 minutes.

Punch dough once in center and remove from bowl, divide in two and place each half on a greased cookie sheet. To form a skull, form dough into an oval shape, with a greased knife, cut two horizontal slits for eyes, one vertical slit for a nose and one horizontal slit for the mouth. Gently pull apart the dough, with greased fingers, so you can see the pan below. Cover and let rise to 75% of double.

After the dough has risen, uncover and reopen eyes, nose and mouth holes. You can brush dough with beaten egg white before baking if desired.

Bake for 25 minutes. Remove from baking sheet immediately and butter or oil all sides of the bread. Let cool slightly before serving.

YouTube video at the following link:
http://www.youtube.com/watch?v=YZkh27ZHzEk

Dipping Sauce / Glaze (optional)

A perfectly sweet addition to your completed bread. Prepare this while your bread is baking.

Ingredients:
- 1 bar or tub of cream cheese or cream cheese substitute softened
- Powdered sugar
- Vanilla

Warm cream cheese in microwave or pan, add powdered sugar until you get a smooth consistency, add flavoring. Serve bread with dipping sauce.

YouTube video at the following link:
http://www.youtube.com/watch?v=ApNMUJmif6Y

Flax Eggs or Egg Substitute

This is a wonderful substitute for eggs, if you are vegan or if you are simply out of eggs. They even have a slimy consistency of eggs, though I would not recommend scrambling them.

- 1/3 cup milled flax seed
- 1 cup water

Mix thoroughly in a bowl and let sit. Once the mixture reaches egg like consistency, it is ready to use.

3 Tbs = 1 whole egg
Makes enough for six eggs

Sugar Skulls

These sweet treats look tasty but are not edible. This is a traditional recipe used to celebrate the "Day of the Dead" that is used to create effigies of loved ones that have passed on. The whole family can gather together and create little remembrances of those who have gone before us.

Ingredients:
- 4 to 5 cups powdered sugar
- 1 egg white
- 1 Tbs corn syrup
- 1/2 tsp. vanilla
- Cornstarch
- Food coloring
- 1 new unused water color paintbrush
- Large plastic bag
- Large container

In a large bowl, mix the egg white, corn syrup, and vanilla in a clean bowl until all incorporated. Mix in the powdered sugar, about two cups at a time, until a dough ball forms and the dough is no longer wet looking. Remove dough from bowl and knead on a hard surface that has been dusted with powdered sugar. Keep kneading until dough is firm and stiff.

Put about 1 cup of corn starch in the large plastic bag. Form dough into 1 inch balls and coat with starch by dropping the ball into the starch filled bag. Place starch coated balls into a large container. Cover container tightly with plastic wrap and refrigerator overnight.

When ready to form skulls, take sugar ball and cup in hands for about 5 to 10 seconds to warm slightly, so it will not crack while shaping. When ball becomes slightly pliable, form your skull.

Set on tray and let dry overnight.
Decorate with food coloring.

YouTube video at the following link:
http://www.youtube.com/watch?v=yRGSVbFO0Cg

Samhain Sabbat – Full Ritual

Items for ritual:

- One small gold taper candle
- One small silver taper candle
- Black cloth for altar covering
- A vase of mums
- Enough apples for each person in circle

- Parchment with a list of things each person wants to banish (have participants do this beforehand)
- White votive candle
- Cauldron with a black tea light inside
- Patchouli oil
- Apple cider
- Sweet skull bread
- Usual ritual items

Insert into ritual circle format

Ring bell:

"Behold the season of Samhain, the final harvest of the year. We have gathered your bounty great Goddess to prepare for the dark stillness of winter. Thank you for the plentiful harvests."

Light the black candle in the cauldron:

As participants hold their parchment, say:

"This is the time we enter into the darkest part of the year and so the depths of our souls become ever present. As we reflect on all aspects of ourselves there is much we have chosen to release to the great Goddess. As you prepare to cast away what no longer serves you, think about all you have to look forward to without these burdens on your shoulders."

Have participants burn their list in the flames of the candle. Have them imagine all these feelings evaporating into smoke as they say:

"In this cauldron of endings and new beginnings, I cast all my burdens into your belly of death. By releasing these things to you great Goddess, I am free of them. So Mote It Be."

Anoint the white votive candle with patchouli oil:

"Tonight the veil is very thin and the door to the other realms are wide open for all to pass through. We honor those who have gone before us and thank them for the sacrifices that they have made for future generations. As we light this candle we welcome all ancestor spirits this Samhain night. Welcome."

Put candle in window of your home after ritual for the Spirits.

Hold hands with everyone in the circle and say:

"As we dance and spiral, we celebrate these gifts and honor the womb of the Goddess from which we all have come from. We also honor the God, the beloved lover of the Goddess from which this harvest was seeded."

Have two people drop one hand from each other, to create a gap. Have one person be the start and the other is the ending of the dance line. The person acting as the beginning, start to dance in a spiral until everyone is close and cannot move. Then have the end become the beginning and spiral out to form a circle again.

"The God has gone back to the Goddess, to her loving cauldron of rebirth."

Put out the God candle and put the God Statue under the altar (signifying his death).

Have each person in circle hold up an apple to the direction of above:

"We call upon the Goddess to bless these apples and all the spirits who visit and partake of them tonight. The apple, whose center is a perfect pentagram, is a perfect symbol of all of creation from the beginning of time to the present. Blessed Be."

(Leave apples outside for the spirits)

[Finish ritual with the format chosen from chapter 2]

~ Notes ~

~ Notes ~

~ Notes ~

Chapter 11

Simple Sabbat Cookies

These simple and light cookies are a perfect addition to your Sabbat ritual. They can be used for the "cakes" portion of the ritual or for any day of the year.

Ingredients:
- ¼ cup shortening
- ¼ cup butter or butter substitute softened
- ¾ cup granulated sugar
- 1/3 cup milk (soy, cow, goat or almond. Do not use rice milk, it doesn't come out correctly.)
- 1 tsp pure almond extract
- 1 Tbs pure vanilla extract
- 2 cups flour
- 1 ½ tsp baking powder

Preheat oven to 350°F. Cream together first three ingredients. Add remaining ingredients and mix with spoon or hand mixer. Roll dough out to ¼ of an inch thickness on a floured surface and cut into shapes.

Sabbat shape ideas:

- Candlemas – Flames or candles
- Ostara – Eggs or rabbits
- Beltane – Flowers
- Summer Solstice – Suns
- Lammas – Fruits, pumpkins, leaves, or veggies
- Mabon - Apples, pumpkins or baskets
- Samhain – Cauldron, witches hat, or apples
- Yule – Evergreen trees, Suns or stars

Bake at 350°F for 8 - 9 minutes on an ungreased cookie sheet, until cookies are golden brown on bottom and edges are set. Remove from sheet and carefully transfer to racks or paper towels to cool.

YouTube video at the following link:
http://www.youtube.com/watch?v=0TIGta8yYag

~ Notes ~

~ Notes ~

A Wonderful Resource

Goddess College

For women who would like to explore their divine connection to the Goddess and the feminine blood mysteries this is the place for you. Z. Budapest offers training in Tarot, Herbs, Self-Discovery and much more. The Goddess College also offers Clergy programs in the Dianic tradition.

www.GoddessCollege.com

For men who would like to explore their mysteries please visit:

http://cayacoven.org/botm.html

Other Products and Services Available From the Author

FloraSage Therapies

Flora's personal business started in 1997 as HomeCEO, a company that did home organization and energetic space clearing. Today Flora offers much more. Her signature package, The Yay Factor™ life coaching program is her most popular program in which Flora partners with her clients to help create the life they have always dreamed of. Flora offers a 53 week *Year and a Day* Pagan study program for those who find Flora's method of teaching appealing. She also offers intuitive readings over the phone as well as mindful meditation sessions, Shamanic services (available upon request) and is also a workshop facilitator and presenter. Flora is also trained in Sound healing and is a Certified Tuning Fork Therapy® Practitioner. Flora is available for special events, interviews and retreats.

Visit Flora at her website for upcoming events and promotions. Sign up for her newsletter. You can also connect with Flora on Twitter and Facebook from her website:

www.FloraSage.com

CharmingPixieFlora

Flora's personal teaching channel on YouTube is an eclectic mix of Pagan studies, crafts, daily living and life coaching strategies for people from every walk of life. Her balanced approach to living is a constant source of empowerment for those who wish to watch.

Visit Flora at her YouTube channel:

http://www.YouTube.com/user/CharmingPixieFlora

Food Magic

Food Magic – Herbal Healing Through Conscious Divine Intent

Flora Peterson and Bobbie Grennier have partnered with Z. Budapest to create a powerful series of *Food Magic* DVDs for women everywhere. It incorporates the magical and medicinal properties of food stuffs and traditional methods of cooking that will have your group craving more with each lesson.

Food magic is a woman honoring series of social cooking projects which can be done by women and men alike, but harkens back to a time when women came together socially to prepare meals and enjoy a spiritual connection to the divine while creating nourishment and healing concoctions. Since this is woman honoring, we focus on the divine Goddess as existed in Matriarchal times as influencing the magical intent behind what we cook and why. It's the creation and enjoyment of food with a higher purpose!

Food Magic is a coming together of the magical properties of all the ingredients with the herbal healing properties, and a blessing for recipes from Z Budapest.

We make all the recipes from scratch and the ingredients are from scratch as well. For example, if a recipe calls for ketchup, we will be making that from scratch instead of just buying a bottle of ketchup. We do this because we want you to know exactly what's in your food and how it affects you magically and healthfully.

Plus, when women come together to make all their own all natural food, it is life-affirming. Culturally we women need time to nurture ourselves and each other ... and what better way to share that experience than through Food Magic!

Food Magic and Natural Herbal Healing just go together and we think you'll have A LOT OF FUN and GOOD TIMES with our creative and easy to do projects.

Why it's perfects for groups!

We work closely with women's spiritual leader Z Budapest, and she's told us that women desire to host women's group events in their homes, but often lack the time of preparing an activity for their friends. Many times those events never happen because the hostess is overwhelmed. That's where Food Magic comes in!

We decided to create a fully prepared series of social events that you can use right out of the box. We will provide you will everything you need, minus the ingredients.

146

Here's what Food Magic gives you:

- A *grocery list* of all ingredients needed for each group event
- *Recipes* that provide you with ingredients and detailed cooking instructions.
- A description of *magical properties* for all ingredients.
- A description of all *herbal healing properties* for all ingredients.
- A *CD* with all the documents (recipes and grocery lists) in PDF for easy printing.
- A *DVD* with videos showing you and your friends exactly how to make everything.
- Plus, Z Budapest *herself* giving you the blessings and spiritual intent for each recipe.
- And your own beautiful *Food Magic apron*!

Please visit Food Magic on the web at:

http://www.food-magic.com/

To Write to the Author

If you wish to contact the author or would like more information about this book, interviews or any other inquiries, please write to the following address:

M. Flora Peterson
c/o FloraSage Therapies
P.O. Box 2286
Owasso, OK 74055 U.S.A.

http://www.FloraSage.com

Made in the USA
San Bernardino, CA
19 April 2015